MW00526308

Growing Gardens

—

Growing People

Growing Gardens

—

Growing People

Creating The Great School Garden Volume I

Mason Vollmer

Copyright © 2015 Mason Vollmer

Photographs © 2015 Mason Vollmer

All rights reserved. No part of this publication may be reproduced, stored
in a retrieval system, or transmitted in any form or by any means,
electronic, mechanical, photocopying, recording, scanning, or otherwise,
except as permitted under Section 107 or 108 of the 1976 United States
Copyright Act, without written permission of the Author.

ISBN-13: 2 978-0-9967168-0-2

DEDICATION

To Celia Chase Mason Vollmer, who
encouraged me to keep country values alive

ABOUT THE AUTHOR

Mason Vollmer grew up in Palo Alto, CA, where he was introduced to Biodynamic gardening by author, gardener, and researcher John Jeavons, and Master Gardener Alan Chadwick, through the Saratoga Community Garden and the Covelo California Garden.

He studied Soil Science at Cal Poly San Luis Obispo. Biodynamic Agriculture, Rural Development, Anthroposophy, and Waldorf Education at Emerson College in Sussex, England.

Educational gardens, which he has helped to grow include:

Camp Joy–Boulder Creek, CA

Kainos Work Activity Center–Redwood City, CA

Summerfield Waldorf School–Santa Rosa, CA

Kimberton Waldorf School–Kimberton, PA

Camphill Soltane–Glenmoore, PA

CONTENTS

Introduction

Why Gardening Is More Than I Thought It Was

I love sharing with young people how to grow fragrant flowers and herbs, tasty crisp veggies, and how to make awesome compost from "waste." Yet, nothing compares to growing confident, capable children. Over time, I've come to realize the most important thing we grow in the school garden is the human spirit itself.

Whether you are a teacher, parent, farmer, or gardener, you are involved in growing people, and that includes yourself. And if you have the opportunity to create a school garden or already have a school garden and looking for tips, this book is filled with practical ideas for you, gathered over decades of horticultural education experience.

A good school garden is like having an adjunct teacher at your side. One of the most valuable lessons, I've learned in horticulture education, is the same garden activity means different things to different age groups. This means you don't need to create a

1

separate "postage stamp" garden for each class, since each group will take away a lesson appropriate to their age.

This makes your work significantly easier. Still, there is always room for new projects as the children grow, and each sees what their siblings, friends, and classmates, are working on, and looking forward to with anticipation, or look back on as they recollect in the future.

In the first chapter of the book, I will share an overview of a 6-part garden curriculum from elementary, through middle school, and into high school. There is almost no subject that cannot be related in some way to gardening. Gardening is an ancient, primary human activity, a metaphor for community, and our role as caretakers for the earth, and one another.

There are many challenges to creating a great school garden. Most of these challenges can be solved by: good design, seasonal planning, and people skills. You will create a great school garden by applying these strategies in your school and community.

Although I have worked in 12 educational gardens, I will focus here on my experiences from a single 2-acre school garden I established at a private K-12 school. Like a farmer looking over the fence, and gaining ideas from next door...take what makes sense to you and apply it to your garden.

In a second volume, I will focus on *Growing Gardens* with adults, who have developmental differences. Here we will move beyond the art and academics of gardening, towards the vocation of horticulture.

This approach creates future opportunities to include people with developmental differences, in joining a new "guild of horticulturalists," who grow food, flowers, and herbs, organically in urban settings.

—Mason Vollmer

1 What Is Gardening For?

Lessons in a School Garden

School gardens can reinforce a wide range of subjects, including these six broad areas:

1) **Humanities/History/Geography**–Many different regions and cultures have specific crops, celebrations, and traditions, reaching back into the domestication of plants and animals.

2) **Art/Therapeutic**–Gardening can provide many benefits that complement head knowledge including practical hands-on skills, and heart skills that are connected with beauty, caring, and compassion.

3) **Sciences**–Lessons usually taught in labs can find real context in the garden, including physics, mechanics, math, and chemistry.

Environmental and Earth Sciences have already burst out of the confines of an academic arena and entered the social/ political sphere.

4) **Health/Nutrition**–Often this area is combined with the sciences, yet if there are food/dining facilities in addition to gardening, then practical exercises in experiencing quality foods are possible.

5) **Community Service/Civics**–Depending upon your situation you can bring produce, or volunteer hours out of your classroom and into the community for experiential/service learning.

6) **Entrepreneurial**–Gardening can also offer lessons in creating and delivering value. This kind of value originates in the hands of the craftsman/artist and is very empowering by strengthening the will for work.

Depending upon the individual situation, a gardening program will find its strength in one or more of these areas. A holistic approach to human development, understands that all of humanity, together with our planet, is a garden, worthy of study, service, and devotion.

Although much of my experience in creating school gardens, and programs arose by working in Waldorf education, there are many lessons here that I've used in other community gardens and horticultural programs. Every school is a unique situation with different opportunities and limitations. There is no one-size-fits-all formula for creating a school garden.

The essential point is: What should your garden bring out the most in your students' development? If time allowed, you could bring in all six areas, as the students become ready to learn different lessons.

I don't think the potential for how a school garden can enhance education has been exhausted yet. There is a new generation of garden teachers exploring ways that gardening can re-enliven both the place, and program, in which participants learn.

And after years of growing school gardens, I've learned that in addition to children learning to garden, the whole institution learns something important and valuable when it invites a school garden into its faculty, facility, and community.

You *are* growing: people, the community, and the institution itself, alongside growing your garden. A garden teacher has much to do,

4

in addition to creating lesson plans, writing reports, and attending meetings. You have to build, organize, and maintain your teaching facility—the *living* classroom that is a school garden.

If you are starting, or maintaining, a school garden you are always looking out for ideas around garden organization, age-appropriate activities, tools, projects, cooking and crafting ideas, and more, that fit your situation. Further, there is a modeling quality in teaching and, too, you can learn a lot from your students. Your students are *your* teachers. So pay close attention and they will reveal to you what they need the most. And know that as you garden, your interest and enthusiasm is crucial in awakening their interest in learning what you have to show and share.

You will determine what your school garden's strength will be. From the list of six broad areas listed above, find out what will reach your community and student body best. Every school has it's own culture that evolves slowly over time out of interaction between faculty and students.

Today, its seems there is less time for the traditional foundation of a liberal arts education that the first three areas focus on. Yet Waldorf education keeps these as central to its main lesson curriculum. The second three areas offer powerful garden opportunities for urban schools, often with tight budgets, to focus on health, community service, and jobs.

Ask yourself: What is gardening for? Then set up your school garden to be rich in activities that reveal those outcomes for your students. You will then awaken something genuine that empowers your students to become learners that love to learn, and gardeners who love to garden and are transformed by doing so.

During times like ours, when economic, social, and environmental challenges shake our future, we would be wise to build school gardens that nurture the whole human being in body, soul, and spirit. In all traditional cultures, the gardener tends both the earth and the community.

In this way, we grow gardens to grow caring people—That's what the garden is for.

2 A Place In Time

One September Day

On a Wednesday afternoon in September, a group of sixth graders came up to the garden for a gardening class. As the students arrive, I'm picking chamomile blossoms and those first to arrive are eager to help out. By the time everyone has arrived, we have about four cups of sunny, yellow and white, slightly sticky, pineapple-smelling blossoms.

The cone shaped centers are what we are going for, and with many hands it takes less than ten minutes to separate them out. At the end of class, I will put these precious flowers in a dehydrator to capture their essence, and keep them in tight containers (zip lock bags are fine), until we are ready to make an herbal tea blend, a good rainy-day activity.

With all the students present (there is an occasional late-comer, music lesson etc.), we gather on benches in the center of the garden and I greet the class saying, "Good afternoon, sixth grade," and they chime back, "Good afternoon, Mr. Vollmer." Then I give a little preview of what we will be doing today: harvesting some onions planted last April and drying some flowers. Both were started during the previous school year, when everyone was a grade lower.

All this will be set aside for future projects; the onions will keep a while, until they can be sliced, dried, and stored, to later make a savory, herb salt. The drying flowers will be bunched and hung to completely dry, upside down in the classroom, for later use when small bouquets and boutonnieres can be made for Advent, Christmas, and Valentine's Day.

When I started teaching gardening third-through-tenth grade, I originally thought of individual projects for specific grades, but in practice came to find that the interweaving of time, projects, and different age groups, required a different approach. Rather than having garden plots dedicated to a particular class, a kind of community garden approach emerged, where every class might have a hand in the herb garden at some time. Yet this time in the garden meant different things to different grades.

School gardens can have a kind of magical effect that allows each student to get what they need from it. If the teacher is alert and open to the moment, you can bring out the lesson best suited for that moment and age group. In practice, this means you over prepare, but you need to let that all go, and live in the moment, doing what needs doing in the garden right then and that's right for that season, while remembering how the past prepared this moment, and how what we do today, sets something aside for tomorrow and for others.

After telling the students that we will harvest onions and dry flowers, I tell the students to get baskets and gloves (optional, most want to really touch the soil, particularly the younger ones, others must have gloves), the students go to the tool shed where they have been divided into four different groups. At the first garden class in September, I made a point of assigning the students into one of four tool groups, so we can get and put away tools efficiently, and that way the next class can do the same.

With four benches in our gathering area, this made it easy. I prepared a clipboard for each bench, which is color-coded: red, yellow, blue, and orange, and then students sign up by writing their names in the assigned pencil color. If I need to adjust the numbers in each group, which is typically 3-5 students per group, I do that while on the benches, then we go to the tool shed, where four sets of color-coded tools are kept, hang up our clipboards, and get the tools we need. Then when you see that the red group has left a tool out, you can more easily ask someone in that group to put it away and develop responsibility towards our tools and workspace.

Outdoor gathering area to begin and end classes

Then we bring our tools to the onion bed. First, I demonstrate what we need to do: pull the onion, brush off any soil, and put them into the basket. Four areas are marked out for each group. In laying out the garden, I learned to alternate beds with cover crops, mulch, or grass, to act as easy access rows to our currently-cropped beds. After a bed is harvested, it is put into a cover crop, and what was an access path becomes the next season's bed.

This has a dual purpose: providing access for students, wheelbarrows, and baskets, and improving garden soil by rotating crops, adding organic matter through cover crops, mulches, and grass sod. I used a measurement of 5' for each bed. This can be measured from center-to-center or edge-to-edge. When the garden is located in a block, this helps to keep track of beds, and crop rotation histories for record keeping. Another popular way is to use raised beds. In a smaller setting, this is a good way to go, as it's always surprising how much path space you need when working with larger groups. For a garden teacher, it can be shocking how quickly students can work, and inwardly you wonder if they really got it, but you'll find they did, and in ways that are not immediately obvious.

Starting right away with my youngest class, the third grade, I emphasize the important thing is that we work together and help each other out. Sometimes at the beginning, or at the end of a class, I will tell a short story of when a neighbor farmer helped me out and that's how it is in farming communities. At harvest time everyone has harvest fever, and if you finish first, and you see your neighbor struggling, you jump in and help. Perhaps someday they'll return the favor, when your wagon is broken and you're struggling, or weather threatens.

Then we set the onions in a warm dry place to "harden off." And since our tool shed is actually a modified greenhouse, there are shelves in there for just this purpose. Whereas the flowers we are about to harvest need to be hung up out of the sunlight, I find that the classroom is a perfect place for this. Once we have transferred our onions to nursery flats, we get hand clippers and take our baskets to the dry flower garden and harvest some strawflower, statice, gomphrena, and other flowers particularly suited for drying.

Actually they feel dry already, but will dry and harden into rather brittle, everlasting flowers that can be crafted later into wreaths, bouquets, or boutonnières. I use rubber bands to form and hold the bunches of flowers, and little S-shaped hooks made out of a short piece, about 3" to 4", of vinyl coated electrician's wire. You can get a big spool cheaply at any hardware store. The S-shaped

9

hooks allow me to hang the bunch on a twine strung up high in the classroom. It's rather pretty to look up and see an upside-down flower from the garden looking back down at you.

As the flowers dry out they can shatter and fall apart easily, so smaller bunches are easier to dismantle later for projects and the rubber bands contract as the flowers shrink, holding them in place better than twine. As they dry, they can be transferred to cardboard storage boxes or sometimes I use the large paper bags used in the fall for leaf clean up. Since both cardboard and paper breath nicely, they are less likely to mildew than plastic. Although if they are dry enough, clear storage containers can work, but with our high humidity, paper is safer.

All the while, the garden teacher is keeping close track of time. Timing is a real art, although the students may come late to your class, you had better not send them too early or too late to their next class or you'll create friction among your colleagues. So with the last 5-10 minutes left, we get a drink of water (or best of all, have a snack from the garden, a fresh carrot, popcorn, or iced herb tea) near our gathering area.

We then take a seat and I reflect back to them what they've accomplished, and how grateful I am for their efforts, while reminding them that these onions were planted by last year's sixth grade (now big seventh graders), and how we will later use the onions to prepare an herb salt that can be used to season: popcorn, french fries, pasta, or other savory dishes that we might prepare on cold winter days with produce from the garden. I also share how we will use the dry flowers to make wreaths and other items for the Craft Show in December.

This sums up, how we often harvest what others have sown, and how the work we do today benefits others tomorrow. The past and future meet in the work of today in big ways and small.

Working with nature, awakens a community spirit that ultimately connects us with the whole world. I close by saying, "Goodbye and thank you, Class Six," and they all chime back, "Goodbye and thank you, Mr. Vollmer."

Whatever age the students are, there are age appropriate ways in which gardening can support their current developmental stage. The same activity can connect differently, depending upon the age of the class and their developmental readiness. Therein lies the art of education: knowing the right question, or activity, in the moment that will open their soul to wonder, interest, and discovery.

3 Garden Design – A Mosaic of Places

Children are often unaware of the seasons. They first meet the garden as a place, and later learn about the river of time and the seasons, in which life lives.

Before I give a list of possible work stations within a school garden, let's touch on the basics: fencing and irrigation. It's terrible to have your work, and more importantly your student's work, devoured by wildlife. Our culture, and particularly our suburbs, is way out of balance with nature and wildlife.

Fencing is your best strategy to secure your efforts. My fence has saved us from deer, rabbits, and even a loose dairy bull from a neighboring farm, once. Raccoons and ground hogs present another level of assault. With some research, I found a fence company in a county over, Lancaster, that put up 1,200 feet, of 8' tall, game fence in two days for $6,000. A third of the price that other local fence companies here in suburban Chester County wanted.

A fence also reinforces a sense of place with boundaries; yet, until plantings grow in, it can look rather stark. A school garden is different than a picnic or play area, as it is an intentional outdoor classroom that supports specific lessons and activities. When you enter a music room, or an art studio, you want to feel a creative spirit invites you to take creative action.

Garden design can follow specific activities, such as: here we make compost, grow herbs, store tools, sow seeds, etc. From this arises, something we might call "place memory." Children know this from a sandbox, for instance. When they return to the sandbox they often pick up where they left off in their play.

Similarly, my classes often follow a pattern, even though actual activities vary over the course of the year: 5-10 minutes gathering, greeting, and introduction, followed by 1 or 2 activities ~20 minutes each, and closing, perhaps with something from the garden, like a carrot or fruit.

It is nice when the students can receive something from nature each week and so develop a kind of indebtedness and gratitude towards nature and the work of others. Often at least three areas come into play in any given class. It's important to have a good dismissal. Thank your students, and shake hands individually as they leave.

Include areas that involve activities that you are particularly passionate about, for example dye plants and so on. The students draw a great deal from your inner attitude towards things, in ways that are not always obvious. Each day, prepare yourself with patience, caring, and curiosity. This will act like nourishment for your students, yourself, and the activity.

Dedicated areas include: • Gathering areas (I had a shady one for hot days, as well as a central area.) • Compost shed (Ours was located near the cafeteria, as well as compost bins in the garden.) • Soils yard • Tool shed • Classroom • Storage • Greenhouse/Nursery • Annual beds • Perennial beds • Herb garden • Flower garden • Forcing garden • Coppice/Pollard • Fruit trees • Berries • Apiary • Surroundings: Woods, Stream, Campus and Farm

Gathering Areas

Gathering areas can be created using benches that can convert to half picnic tables, and which can also double as project areas, are a great way of establishing a rhythm and form to your lessons. Sometimes, beginning a lesson sitting down, helps young groups focus and listen to instructions.

Here, at the benches, I meet and dismiss the class, and lay down any ground rules: no running or throwing, etc. This bench area was one of the first areas I worked on. It allowed me to divide classes into four groups easily, focus our beginnings and endings together, and have an area for wrapping bouquets, snacking on carrots, or husking dry corn.

Shady gathering area under pollarded willow

You may see in tool catalogs the "hardware," actually plastic, for constructing these benches from simple 2" x 4" x 8' lumber but I used 10' length (against the manufacturers recommendation) to accommodate more students at a bench.

Nearby, I constructed a watering set-up that allowed 12 students to wash their hands, get a drink, or clean a carrot, from common plumbing supplies, set upon a pair of saw horses, that could be moved to different locations. A special hose, with two female fittings, formed the supply connection to any one of the single faucets.

You can only build it according to your water pressure, as the flow is distributed among the number of faucets. Of course, someone discovers by shutting off all but one faucet produces a fountain. Which can be refreshing on a hot day...or get you in trouble.

Compost Shed

How big should a garden be? As large as you can take care of well, and this includes being able to make enough compost to fertilize and use for soil mixes. We built a shed especially for turning kitchen and lunch scraps into compost using a large compost tumbler and leaves gathered and stockpiled in the autumn to last all year. Granular lime can be added daily, and a couple of sixth graders had composting as one of their weekly classroom chores on a rotational basis after lunch.

We made about 7 yards of really great, nearly-weed-seed-free compost for our nursery potting mixes. Also composting can occur in open bins, without the top or bottom on, throughout the garden, to minimize hauling distances. I made a series of nesting modular composting bins out of cedar and 1/4" hardware cloth. They had a bottom, and a lid, and could be stacked one, two, or three high, as shown in the photo.

A big activity in October is raking and hauling leaves in order to stockpile enough carbon material to mix with the nitrogen-rich kitchen and lunch scraps, for a good carbon/nitrogen balance. The stretchers shown earlier, can be laid flat and leaves raked right on for hauling to the pile.

Soils Yard

A soils yard is for sifting and blending soil mixes, for making cuttings and filling containers. You can buy soil mixes of course, but there is great satisfaction to be found in making your own mixes and experiencing the different qualities and properties of compost, sifted soil, perlite, vermiculite, peat moss, and coconut coir.

Our simplest mix was just 3 parts sifted compost to 1 part perlite. Find yourself a wholesale nursery supplier, who services local garden centers, and set up an account for direct delivery of horticultural supplies like perlite, pots, labels, etc. Perlite is a natural mineral, which is baked, or puffed, to create a very porous, light-weight sand. But the dust should be avoided.

This garden is on a slope. Just below the wheelbarrows are bins cut into the hillside for holding sifted compost, perlite, and other soil mix materials. Boards are covering the bins, that can be filled from above and accessed from below, next to a shaded work bench.

I put 1 part perlite into a wheelbarrow, place the 1/4" sieve on top prior to a class coming and they would sieve the compost on top, smothering the dust potential. A 1:3 perlite/compost blend is great for many uses.

Tool Shed

The tool shed for a school garden is a bigger project than what a typical gardener might have. Ideally, there is a place for everything and everything in its place. At a glance, you can see that someone left a pair of loppers out, for instance. I made four, color-coded groups: red, yellow, blue, and orange, and painted a color blaze on each tool to help each group and individual gain greater responsibility for their tool care.

Tools are expensive and cheap tools are not recommended; they frustrate the children, break, and are generally discouraging. Schools can sometimes use part of their state funds for tools. Check with your purchasing person about funds used for text books and athletic supplies, and you may find an approved state vendor for hand garden tools. Each year, I tried to add a new set of 16 hand tools and eventually had a great assortment. It's easiest when everyone is doing the same task with the same tools: one demonstration informs the whole group quickly. As they mature, there can be more varieties of tools used simultaneously, to move a multi-step project forward.

My tool shed went through several incarnations as the program developed and moved to its permanent home on the hill over looking the athletic fields. For a time, it was a hoop house, 14' x 48', that doubled as a rainy-day workshop before the classroom was built. During this phase, I had four 12' x 7' bays for each of the four tool groups. I had a clipboard with the weekly schedule and a spot for each class member, fifth grade through tenth grade, to write their name in, so if I saw a red rake left out, I could quickly say, "Aaron, can you check and see if we left a red rake out?"

Often, after meeting in the gathering area and describing and/or demonstrating the task for that day, the next step would be to get the tools needed. And, later, to return them to their places. The next class, just minutes after this one, might need different tools. Some days, the highlight of achievement was being able to get and return tools correctly even if all of the planned garden activities didn't go as envisioned, or the energy of the class was off that day.

When we remember that the goal of every lesson involves awakening a sense of caring and responsibility, then sometimes you have to ditch your plans, and deal with bullying, social dynamics, and meet your students where they are at and search for a better place together.

Classroom

For years, our plastic greenhouse doubled as a tool shed and rainy-day work space. This was awkward, to say the least. Eventually, we built a garden classroom with the help of parents, staff, faculty, and the greater community. This was vital in deepening our connection with nature through cooking, crafting, the sciences, as well as gardening.

It really makes relevant, connections between society and nature, when you can do a project, not in isolation but in context, such as keeping bees and making beeswax candles. Even if you purchase beeswax bulk so you don't raid your own hives too much, the students will know what a precious material beeswax is. Combine that with botany, earth science, meteorology, etc., and we start to see how hands-on learning enriches traditional academic subjects.

The classroom provided many things we didn't have before, including restrooms, a kitchen, patio with outdoor sink, and counter space, storage, a small office, and telephone. The classroom was named *The Samuel Wheeler Morris Building for Gardening and Earth Studies*. Sam was a founding board member from 1941-1988.

The Samuel Morris Wheeler Building for Gardening and Earth Studies

As a representative in the Pennsylvania State House, he authored and passed the first Agriculture Conservation Easement legislation protecting farmland in perpetuity. This was the topic of a whole 10th grade lesson on land preservation.

Storage

All classrooms lack adequate storage, and this is especially true for gardening. Throughout the year, summer and winter, sufficient storage space is always wanting. An outdoor area where bulk items, mulch, lumber, posts, wire, etc., can be stored out of view, yet easily accessed, is vital. Every farm or nursery usually has a utility yard, barn or back lot, where nursery containers and seasonal equipment can be stored with limited access. Indoor storage space for perishables, dried herbs, flowers, fruits, and tools/supplies, is essential in order to carry out activities over the course of the year, when crafting and cooking help fill in during the winter months when outdoor work is limited.

Greenhouse/Nursery

I got advice, early on in my gardening teaching, that suggested I avoid the artificiality of the greenhouse and stay close to nature and the seasons. I was told the students would bring rain gear and indoor alternatives would not be needed. I get the intention, but practically speaking, a large greenhouse that can accommodate groups of students is a boon in a culture (largely urban) that starts the academic year when the growing season is ending, and ends when the growing season begins.

This is a whole topic unto itself with many ramifications, but suffice it to say, for many parents and students, gardening is but a small "add-on" in the scope of all the other subjects and academic pressures facing young people. Often, gardening acts as a therapeutic break from too much head work.

When you work/play/create with your hands, you give your brain a refreshing break. It's almost as good as a nap. So having a greenhouse keeps the horticultural work going, allowing you to over-winter tender herbs and flowers, as well as to start seedlings so the garden may be fully planted, before the school year ends. School may end in June, but people start to check out in May.

As early as January or February, you might want to start sowings of seeds, so you can have good-sized transplants when things warm up. With big transplants, you can reduce weed pressures, as your intended crop quickly fills up the garden bed. I try to have the entire garden planted by June 1st as end of year trips, plays, and reports, cut in on everyone's time. High tunnels and/or a cool greenhouse, can add an entire climate zone warmer, with little or no additional heat, helping you get a jump on the season.

We had a small, multi-functional greenhouse with: a clay stove for cooking and heating, black barrels filled with water for thermal mass, hanging baskets, and fire wood.

Annual Garden Beds & Cover Crops

Annual garden beds are the bread and butter of most gardens, where tomatoes, onions, potatoes, corn, squashes, beans, carrots, herbs, flowers, and more, are grown in rotation.

I can't overemphasize, enough, the use of cover crops to restore, build, and maintain fertility, in annual beds. Some organic growers recommend that 50-75% of your annual beds should be in restorative cover crops. In winter, sow a rye/vetch cover crop over as much, if not all, annual beds. In summer, use buckwheat, clover, or annual rye, in paths, or as crops come out.

There is a beautiful lesson in this. As much as 97% of the biomass in a cover crop comes not from the soil, but from the air and water! You didn't know you were also gardening the air and water around your garden but you are, and it's essential to sustaining soil health and soil biology. Below are: winter rye/vetch; alternate early beds prepared; secondary beds composted on site; summer buckwheat in-between.

Winter Rye/Vetch being composted as beds are prepared for spring planting. By planting only every other bed with crops, alternating with summer cover crops, you constantly replenishing half your arable land.

Perennial Garden Beds

Perennial garden beds take longer to establish but yield flowers, fruits, and vegetables, earlier in the spring than you could otherwise achieve. I put in one perennial planting a year, with the eighth grade, as a kind of gift back to the school garden. And soon you build up a resource that benefits all the garden classes. Think: horseradish, asparagus & rhubarb, or fruit trees and bushes, bulbs, native pollinator plants, etc.

Herb Garden

In our herb garden, we grow peppermint, lavender, calendula, sage, oregano, thyme, chamomile, lemon grass, comfrey, and stevia. Together with annual herbs, and some wild gathered plants, we make an herb tea blend, a skin lotion, and a seasoned salt.

Flower Garden

Our flower garden includes bulbs, paperwhites, daffodils, hyacinths, and tulips, and Sweet Williams, snapdragons, asters, stocks, larkspur, and other flowers that we will dry. I love flowers and find they can play a great role in the April/May school garden as well as again in winter with the dry flowers.

We pick and wrap bouquets of Sweet Williams, using a moist paper towel, a plastic bag, rubber bands, masking tape, and marking pens to make bouquets that travel home with students in May.

Forcing Garden

You may not know about "forcing branches" to flower in spring, but often, when there is still snow on the ground and frosty weather threatening, branches can be cut that will open and bloom indoors in a vase. Our forcing garden doubles as a hedge row and includes magnolia, forsythia, flowering quince, and prunus, which is the peach, cherry, plum, and apricot tree family.

This is similar to making flower bouquets to take home or spread around campus in May. It's also a great way to break out of the doldrums of winter and get a jump on a new season.

Coppice/Pollard

Coppicing and pollarding is also little known, but like forcing branches for early bloom, helped me come up with activities in March. We grow four species of willow: basket willow for crafting; hybrid willow for firewood; pussy willow for flowers; and weeping willow for crafting into willow stars.

Severe pruning to ground level is called "coppicing" and is done February to March. Coppicing is a severe pruning done above "deer height," at the same time. This annual harsh pruning rewards the gardener with a consistent supply of willow wood of a particular diameter. A renewable source of carbon-neutral fuel, it is grown as supplemental heat for our greenhouse, as the carbon released in burning is captured in annual regrowth.

A word of caution, if you start a coppice, you must continue with an annual cutting, or it simply becomes a tree line. Here, coppiced willow canes are woven into a fence for wind protection. Stones from the garden mulched the willow coppice.

Fruit Trees

We planted apple, pear, prune, walnut, almond, pecan, and chestnut, including two apple tunnels. These were part of the eighth grade perennial projects. And a "Belgian fence" espalier apple trellis. For years, I taught espalier: the art of training fruit trees. This deserves a book on it's own. Long story short, I now recommend the "Tall Spindle" system using dwarfing rootstocks and disease resistant varieties.

I am currently running a horticulture program for adults with developmental differences, and we have found the high-density, dwarf apple system to be accessible, productive, and easy to care for. This together with an accessible, container growing system forms the basis of Volume II, *Growing Gardens: Good Work For Good People*.

Berries

Autumn bearing raspberries can be pruned in such a way as to delay fruiting past August and into September, when the children return to school. There is also an autumn-bearing, thornless blackberry, Freedom, that bears very late on new growth in September. Strawberries fruit after school is out in late June, so I haven't put a lot of effort into them, but there is great work being done with containers and overbearing varieties, including Eversweet that takes the heat well.

Apiary

I built a raised platform so the bees' flight pattern would not interfere with student traffic and they could be viewed more easily. There are few things more exciting than catching a wild swarm in May with students.

Surroundings: Woods, Streams, Campus, & Farm

The woods, streams, campus plantings, and farm surrounding the Kimberton Waldorf school garden provide a wealth of interest and lessons. In the fall, I take the botany class for observation walks and to collect materials for sketching in their main lesson books or making rubbings. With the earth science class, we often follow the path and watershed pattern of a creek that runs through the campus.

In October a great quantity of oak, maple, and other leaves are collected for adding to the kitchen compost. This carbon source compliments the nitrogen-rich kitchen scraps and is rich in microorganisms beneficial to soil and compost development. We also gather wild hickory nuts from the woods in years when they are plentiful.

Across the street is the Biodynamic Seven Stars Dairy, which makes yogurt and raises nearly all its feed on site. Here we can see the cows, newborn calves, and exemplary land stewardship. One year, an apprentice at the dairy brought his draft oxen over regularly for chores, hauling manure with eager third graders.

4 Seasons—Rhythms of Nature and the Academic Year

Another September Day

September is the richest month in a school garden year. One challenge for the garden teacher is that it goes by too quickly. The theme for the month is: *Harvest–Capture The Sunlight Of Summer For Winter To Come*. Against the background of this activity is a mood quite contrary to the gardener's sense of the season coming to an end; an inner excitement in the children to be a grade older, and an overflowing sense of possibility and potential: new friends, new skills, fresh discoveries. For the gardener, these qualities are more associated with March, and all the dreams of a new growing season. Yet the academic year is September–June.

Here we face the fact, that the school year begins, when the growing season ends, and the school year ends, when the growing season begins. For the novice garden teacher, this can be frustrating. By necessity, I developed strategies to embrace this counter-current of human life and nature. The best gardening example for this is the Native American tradition—The Three Sisters: Corn, Beans, and Squash.

Each gardener should feel free to adapt the Three Sisters' planting approach to fit their situation. There is no one-size-fits-all formula. I've tried different ways of combining the Three Sisters and have found an approach that works for me, although it's different from anything I've read, or seen elsewhere. So we have to step out of this September day, backwards in time, to see how we started these corn beds.

A lot of people don't know that corn can be transplanted. The first time a farmer friend of mine saw my method, I could see he thought I was nuts, which may be a genuine observation. But farming and gardening are different; the farmer can direct sow corn on a big scale in the spring once the soil has warmed and dried out enough. But in a school garden, that would be too late in the school year to get everything planted in time, before school lets out for summer.

And small beds of sprouting grain in a garden are particularly attractive to birds and rodents. With healthy transplants, a garden bed can be quickly established, and mulched to inhibit weed growth getting your beds off to a good start, ensuring that a crop is waiting to harvest in September. That's the other great thing about growing "dry" corn, it's well wrapped from autumn rain and is forgiving about when you get around to harvesting it. It's not a strawberry.

In April, in flats with forty, 2" round cells per tray, with or without peat pots, using our own 3- parts-sifted compost to 1-part-perlite soil mix, we sow one kernel of corn per cell. We save our own strain of Calico popping corn. At the same time, or as much as 2-3 weeks later, we sow Jack Be Little Pumpkins in the same manner, only you need only a quarter to a sixth the number of these plants, as you do of corn.

Sometimes the same class, or an older class, will have filled the flats with soil mix ahead of time. I use an empty flat as a carrying tray to hold enough metal condiment cups or Dixie cups, with seed for sowing. Then every student gets a cup of seed, two students to a tray, and then they put one seed on top of the soil in each cell, row by row. You may demonstrate this before passing out the seed. When *all* the cells have a seed, using your finger, gently press the seed into the soil, to the depth of your first knuckle, and press down the soil around to cover. This way, you *know* each cell got a seed, *before* it gets covered. You don't want to find out a week later that all the seeds went into the first row and three quarters of the tray is empty.

In three to four weeks you will have sturdy little corn plants about 5" tall. During this germination time, the garden beds can be prepared for planting. If the ground is well-prepared, the students can use a planting stick to mark the spots for planting. A planting stick can be configured to give different row spacing; 6", 12", 18" 24" and 30".

A garden bed for corn can be 3 rows, 12" apart, with plants every 12". Two weeks after transplanting, we then direct sow an Amish field bean seed next to every other corn plant. This gives the corn plant enough of a head start. If you plant the bean too early, the corn plant won't be strong enough to provide support for the twining bean plant. You might do a weeding before the bean planting, followed by a good 4" leaf mulch blanketing. Or if the transplants are big enough mulch right away and direct seed the beans right through the mulch.

The beans and corn share the same bed, in the next bed, which also had a winter cover crop, I prepare a squash bed, leaving room for a strong trellis to support the Jack Be Little Pumpkins, which in our Three Sisters garden is the "squash." You can use other winter squashes, but this was most space efficient for our garden, yielding enough mini-pumpkins for students to take them home. I've also used a small ornamental gourd some years and they were a delight. But the great thing about Jack Be Little is, it's a true pumpkin: edible *and* ornamental.

The center from one bed, to the center of another bed, is 5' feet, as is the measure from path to path: symmetry. I alternate current season crops with soil improving cover crops, giving me the option of mowing down the cover crop, leaving a nice 5' access path for students and wheelbarrows during planting and mulching. You can then sprinkle buckwheat seed into the stubble of the path, and have successive crops of biomass enrich what will be next year's cropping bed. If you fill every bed, it leaves only a 14" path and the beds start to get accidentally walked on, or damaged from wheelbarrows and traffic.

"Feed the Soil and the Soil will feed your crops." Much of maintaining soil fertility organically involves nutrient cycling. This means stockpiling leaves in the autumn; cover cropping; composting and aerobic activated compost teas. It's surprising that all the elements you need are all ready present. They just need to be made available through the biology of living soil, composting, and living plants.

Three Sisters: Corn, Beans, and Jack Be Little Pumpkins by third grade students.

Third graders harvest in the fall, and plant another Three Sisters garden the following spring for next year's third grade class. Thus, one class harvests what another has planted, and in turn plants for the next. This, in itself, is a wonderful example of the many inner lessons, hidden within an outwardly simple activity. Like everything in nature and the garden, all is profoundly connected with everything else. You, too, will notice, how much the students have grown since the beginning of the year and when it's time to plant in the spring.

Seven years later, when the students are in the tenth grade, during the Ancient World History block, we will study how the centers of civilization correspond with the discovery of agriculture and grain growing in particular. They will have already had this joyful experience of harvesting and planting, an open-pollinated dry corn, that is passed down from generation to generation and will deeply understand why corn—*Zea maize*—is considered the most highly evolved and specialized plant on the planet.

Spoiler alert: its specific host, essential for its reproduction and survival is *the human being*. Corn is incapable of husking, shelling, and seeding itself, without human intervention. This is the only plant species completely dependent upon human intervention. This exception to the rule could actually prove a new rule: the fate of the entire earth is in our hands. But for now, with the third graders, it's just a lot of fun.

If the schedule allows, and I have the help of an older class, ninth or tenth grade, they know what's coming. I will have set an example of tools near one bed, and with the help of these high school students, we set things up for the third grade, which will be coming to the garden in 15 minutes. Just as with all the garden classes, I divide the high school students among the four benches, and when the third grade comes, they too find their places on the four benches.

Gathered together, I greet the class and give a preview of what's to come, describing what we will do, the importance of safety and cooperation, and where this activity fits into the year's work. Perhaps, rain is forecasted for later in the week, and getting the corn in is important to assure it doesn't rot in the field. Then each bench, in turn, is directed to follow some high school students to a particular corn bed, where different tasks will be demonstrated and assigned to third graders.

The great thing, about growing a dry corn variety, is that it ripens in the fall, at the beginning of the school year, and is not finicky about when it is picked. Unless raccoons get into it, it will wait for you to harvest it. And as with all aspects of gardening with children, it's best if you break tasks down into steps.

This is how we did it. Four teams, using gloves, loppers, stretchers, and a basket and/or a wheelbarrow, would begin to cut down the corn stalks. One student, using the loppers would cut down a stalk. Another student would carry or pass that to a student or two by the stretcher and they would remove any ears of corn, but leave the husk on for today, collecting barren stalks on the stretcher, and putting the ears of corn into the basket or wheelbarrow.

A little bit about the tools. Putting cutting tools in the hands of students always causes a teacher some concern. Safety is always stressed and mentioned at the beginning when demonstrating the task. The great thing about loppers is the distance, between the hands safely gripping the handles, and the cutting area. One needs only to keep the cutting part away from anyone else, carrying them point down and closed, and keeping the blades out of the soil, which can dull the blades.

Corn stalks are thick and need a big tool to cut them. Another approach might be to pull the entire plant up, but then a great deal of soil will cling to the root ball, and it's best to leave the soil in the garden bed. We'll get to what to do with the stalks shortly, but for now we want to safely harvest and store the ears of corn.

The other tool you might not be familiar with is a stretcher. Before I had built up a big collection of tools, I did not have 8 wheelbarrows (expensive!) and yet needed to move things like weeds and leaves, for which a wheelbarrow seemed overkill anyway. So using two 8' boards, I attached a strip of 4' x 6' recycled, tennis court wind fabric that was being discarded, to create something like an old-fashioned ambulance stretcher that could be carried by two or even four people.

This is a very handy tool because it *requires* cooperation to use, and is very versatile. Inevitably students would try and give each other rides, so they need to be constructed strongly, so they can experience this. It lays flat, and weeds or cornstalks, are easily collected and transported in a way that a wheelbarrow just can't. Most wheelbarrows are designed for a man to mix 80 lbs of concrete and deliver it to a site. Yet the wheelbarrow weighs more than a load of leaves or stalks.

At this point, I don't start husking the corn. We've grown a variety of popping corn called Calico for its many beautiful colors, greens, reds, purple, yellow and white, and once you start husking, and seeing all these beautiful colors, you'll never finish clearing the beds. It is both ornamental, and edible as a white popping corn. In spite of its many colors, because the starch inside is white, it pops white and only a small trace of color remains.

Husking can be done indoors later on a rainy day. Some of the Calico husks are a beautiful purple color and an assortment of husks should be saved for making corn dollies. Corn still in- husk can be stored bulk, although there is some moisture in the husk and a small chance of mildew developing.

About two weeks later, we get around to husking. You might want cloth gloves handy, as it can be rough on tender hands. After husking, I store the husked corn in a special can called an incinerator can, which looks like a galvanized metal trash can full of holes. I've lined the interior with window screening so loose kernels don't fall out and to minimize moth traffic. If moths are a big problem, you can bag and freeze shelled or unshelled corn for protection.

Depending upon the size of the group, we might harvest all 8 beds, or save half for another session. Corn stalks are hard and difficult to compost. So after separating the ears of corn from the stalks, we would haul the stalks to an area above future compost piles, where we make a pile for shredding. The BCS tiller, I have, can also operate a shredder. This shredding greatly aids the composting process by exposing more surface area. One could also just use the coarse stalks as a base, upon which a compost pile is built.

During another session, or even with another class, we finish clearing the old corn beds by pulling out the substantial root balls and add them to a compost pile/bin. A heavy-duty garden fork is handy for this task. These too can go in the bottom of a compost pile or the shredder.

During this first autumn work with the corn, the critical task is to secure the harvest. Later, as the entire crop is husked, and the beautiful ears are revealed, the best ears are set aside as seed stock for next year. To ensure a mixed population of Calico popcorn, I make sure a wide representation of colors and ears are included in the seed stock collection.

Then, I take a sampling of kernels from the middle of the ears selected for seed. Since there are ~350 kernels per ear, and two or three ears per plant, one kernel yields 700-1000 kernels. What a multiplication! So it takes only one or two ears worth of kernels to yield nearly 1000 ears. You can also select seed stock prior to harvest, by looking over the crop carefully and selecting ears from plants that have 2 or more ears, are short and stocky to resist wind damage, and you might favor purple husks.

When the husking begins, I use large paper bags, normally sold in the autumn for leaf collection, to store a good supply of cornhusks for crafting into corn dollies in October. Cornhusks are also used in cooking tamales. For that you can buy clean, pressed, dried husks in the ethnic food section of the grocery store, and soak them before using. Or you can set aside your best husks. In humid Pennsylvania, its best to run them through the dehydrator first, and while still dry, bag them up in double-zip freezer bags for storage.

Note: Everyone likes to have cornstalks, pumpkins, and bales of hay to use as decoration around Halloween and as the end of October nears. But the gardener is trying to clear one season away, and prepare for the next, and storage space is always at a premium. Nurseries cut cornstalks, while they are still green to make good-looking ornamental bunches.

Dry corn has "gone too far" to look really good for this, but sometimes I can set aside some good bunches for decoration. In years past, we could cut and haul bunches of corn from our neighboring farmer and construct an open air grass shack, called a Sukkoth, for the Jewish holy day of the same name. I've seen different spellings for Sukkoth.

5 October to June

The Garden in October

It's important to finish clearing the annual beds in order to sow a winter cover crop of a rye/vetch mixture before it gets too cold to germinate. In our zone, that's just after Halloween.

There has been something of a treasure hunt in September, digging late potatoes, and onions. Autumn raspberries have been grazed upon. Corn has been harvested and stored for later projects. Amish dry beans that were set aside to finish drying can later be shelled, cleaned and stored. Jack Be Little Pumpkins and small ornamental gourds have been stored in trays in the greenhouse, now somewhat dry and warm. It's a challenge to hold on to these until the week before Thanksgiving to send home, but it's nice to anticipate that occasion, and set those aside for families so they can see what the children are harvesting in gardening classes.

It took a while for the apples trees to come into bearing, and with small quantities we've been able to slice, peel, and dry. Later as they bore heavier crops, cider, and sauce came into play.

As the harvest theme passes, getting the cover crop of winter rye and winter vetch, on the annual beds is always a weather related dance. Fedco sells a winter cover crop blend that I like, but winter peas and oats are too tender for our harsh winters. Many years the third grade has pulled a small disc harrow, as if a team of draft animals, after standing all in a row and broadcasting the seed over the ground.

October is also the time to have ordered some paperwhite bulbs for forcing, in time for sale at the first Saturday in December, at the Winter Craft Fair. These large bulbs can be potted up singly in 4" pots or trios in a 6" pots using the same soil mix recipe referred to earlier. Keep these moist and in a cool shady place. Low temperatures encourage good root development, while suppressing top growth. 5-6 weeks later, when you bring them to a warmer place, greenhouse or classroom, and they will start to send up leaves and blooms.

Also in September/October, we have set aside dry flowers in bunches. Sometimes after hanging from the ceiling, I set them aside in big paper bags and save half for the Craft Fair, making little boutonnieres as Christmas tree decorations and/or in wreaths, and save the other half for little bouquets around Valentines Day.

If you have a cool greenhouse you can also overwinter other bulbs like freesia, daffodils, hyacinths, and tulips for early container blooms in March/April. Before weather gets bad, its nice to have set aside sifted compost, for continued greenhouse work and early sowings from late January on.

The Garden in November

Our school garden is located above the playing fields and requires a bit of a walk between other classes. The compost shed, however, is located below the playing fields behind the gym and cafeteria. Therefore, on many Autumn days I would intercept the students on their way up, and gather everyone near the compost shed, where we temporarily kept the rakes and stretchers for leaf gathering season. Our campus has many trees and there is an abundance of oak leaves, and more, that can be stockpiled for year-round composting.

Even on a cold day, raking will fast warm you up, and give your upper body a great workout. I like to emphasize that you work with what nature gives you and now its giving leaves: food for the soil and compost. Sometimes we would spend the whole period gathering leaves, and other times just the first half of the class, before continuing on up to the garden for other activities.

Previously, I shared how the compost shed is one of the work stations within the mosaic of places in the school garden, now I want to shift to timing. During this autumn season, nearly all of the carbonaceous materials for composting will be gathered in a 3-5 week season. And some years an early snow shuts this season off before you've collected all you can. The compost shed also comes into use after lunch every day.

All of the lower school classes have a rotating schedule of chores, mostly around caring for their classroom: cleaning, recycling, and so on. For the sixth grade, this includes a couple of students helping to empty bins of kitchen scraps from our organic cafeteria. These nitrogen rich materials need about 3-4 times their volume in leaves. After the grace bell, I supervise this and we empty the bins into the tumbler, add leaves, and lime, and return the bins to the kitchen.

Once a week, I empty the tumbler into a bin placed directly underneath and about once a month, I move the tumbler over a new bin and do little chores around the compost shed on my own. Unlike composting in California, I did not need to water the pile here in humid Pennsylvania. Occasionally, I would add some old compost to act as a cover and/or starter to the bins. So in addition to classes with students, I would spend at least a half hour a week keeping everything in good order around the compost shed.

The Garden in December

Since our school Craft Show (a fund raising event) takes place the first weekend in December, many items have to be prepared in November, such as wreaths, willow stars, paper whites, and small dry flower boutonnieres as tree ornaments. Depending on timing, supplies, and the weather, these activities might continue over into December. Thanksgiving is a big threshold in the garden year, and there is a small window before the craft fair, to pull items together to contribute, as well as for sending home with students.

Regardless of weather, I plan for indoor work during that week between Thanksgiving and Craft Show. You need to be have everything you need for wreath making close at hand. We use willow hoops as the circular base for the wreaths, wire, clippers, raffia, and florists tape. You might have a clear storage box with all you wreath making supplies, in order to save on trips to the craft store. They are likely to run out just when you need things most, so stock up ahead of time. Raffia needs to be soaked about 10 minutes before class starts. Florists tape combines the stickiness of tape with the stretchiness of a rubber band, and doesn't need scissors to cut: all very handy.

You will also need to collect an assortment of greens. Often there are leftovers from the Advent Spiral in the kindergarten. Or I discreetly gather materials from around campus, sometimes with a class, or on my own.

As with many projects, you will make a few examples on your own. This will refresh your memory of the tools, techniques, and time required. Then you come up with a strategy based on your experience of the abilities of each class. When first introducing a project, you might lead the whole class step-by-step, waiting to see that everyone is with you. Then after they get the hang of it, they can proceed at their own pace. This works well when introducing wreath making using a continuous strand of wire to weave everything in a circle around the willow hoop base.

These and other crafting and culinary activities get set up in indoors. This indoor component can serve as a rainy-day activity, or simply a second activity to an outdoor activity. Yet I found it easiest to set up the same indoor activity for nearly all ages, third through tenth grade, and vary the project for the age group. At times, an older class might prepare wreath hoops, or other projects so that a younger class could better use their time and skills.

Indoor and Winter Activities

Gardening is a primary human activity. When we take something from the garden and turn it into something else, we form a bridge between our cultural world and nature. This is how cooking and crafting form a creative continuum that started in nature and reaches fullness in culture. Before we built a classroom with a kitchen, I was limited with what I could do. So we made the most with a clay stove in the greenhouse, as an "indoor" work area. Each year a ninth grade class rebuilt this Lorena Stove that I learned from a Peace Corp volunteer. Some other indoor winter activities include:

Making Corn Dollies

Usually just a third grade activity, but sometimes an older class sees it set up and wants to do it again. Mixing in purple or red husks makes for a nice contrast to the tan husks.

Herb Tea Blend

I found that having two Excalibur dehydrators, with thermostats and timers, essential in preserving herbs in our humid climate. Simply hanging things up was a recipe for decay. I always envisioned clear glass jars with brightly colored herbs...but found zip lock bags more practical. Once somebody drops a jar...or its not sealed properly and goes bad, or needs cleaning, than you find that you have too little time as it is. Pick your battles as it were.

I found plastic wheelbarrows handy in many ways. They are light weight, easy to clean, and I could bring them right into the classroom and load up the dehydrators with the wheelbarrow right below and next to the dehydrator. This was handy, too, when emptying the dehydrator, minimizing spillage.

I also have four sets of soil sieves that are helpful in sieving the herbs to separate the stems from the leaves. Depending upon the volume of materials, we would sieve over trays, large stainless steel bowls, or even the wheelbarrows.

Peppermint, chamomile, and other mints, were the foundation of our tea blend. Add some dried stevia and dried berries and you have a wonderful fruit zinger tea, either hot or cold. This makes a delightful refreshment at the end of a session. Although rather noisy, I used mortar and pestles, and trays from Ikea, so the students could get that hands-on experience of grinding the herbs and mixing it all together. Samples are taken home, as well as a classroom supply. The trays protected the tables and helped keep things tidy. It all feels rather Harry Potter at Hogwarts.

Herb Salt

In contrast to the sweet herbs used in our tea blend, are the savory herbs used for seasoning soups, sandwiches, or popcorn. These include: oregano, thyme, sage, garlic, and mildly hot dried pepper. *Salsa* is a good, mild, sweet-hot variety that won't hurt anyone. Grind these together with a little stevia to get a sweet/hot combo. Garlic is key. You can also dry and grind onion or shallots. Chives are tasty and easy to grow, yet difficult to blend well.

Pies–Pumpkin, Apple, Peach, or Berry

It's always a challenge to arrange a cooking project to fit within say 45 minutes, so you have to make things fit to your situation. This might mean breaking a task down into multiple stages.

Pie filling can be handled different ways, and prepared ahead of time or used fresh. Again it's a time management question. For many years, we had only a small quantity of apples, and they came at a busy time of year. So using the Ikea trays as a work station, together with an apple slicer/corer, little cutting boards, and paring knives (or not) we would prepare apple slices that would go into large bowls of water with a little lemon or anti-browning solution. Then we would dry these slices for later use.

On the day before we needed pie filling, I would reconstitute some of these dry apple slices in white grape juice concentrate and cinnamon, in the fridge overnight, and warm on the stove before class the next day, filling the classroom with a wonderful fragrance anticipating the day's baking project. About 3 tablespoons of filling is all that's needed to make a muffin-sized mini-pie. For pumpkin pies, we often used Butternut squash or pumpkin, that would be halved, baked ahead of time, and the other ingredients added during class for making pumpkin pie filling.

Sometimes, I might make pie crust dough with an older class to set aside for use by a younger class, or use store bought sheets of pie crusts, to speed things along. I use a wide-mouth Mason jar lid to cut out a circle of pie crust. Then I lined a muffin pan to make a dozen mini- pies. Add your filling and bake ~20 minutes in a hot oven and there you go.

For many cooking and crafting projects, I put four large desks together leaving a narrow middle aisle for me (and only me) to slip down and be able to assist four groups. I would then use freezer paper and masking tape to cover the desks to make a clean work surface.

Four groups would make four sheets of mini-pies. I would freeze two or three trays, to bake another day as a winter snack, and save one tray to cool for the next class, and have one tray for sampling. It's all a time management question. If you freeze unbaked pies in the trays, when they are frozen, you can transfer them to freezer bags and use the trays for another class. Therefore, I needed 8 muffin tins if I had two class in a day.

Bread and Pasta

I've never had time to make leavened bread with a class, although it's often the grand conclusion of an eighth grade chemistry block. I just never got it together to fit into a class period. Although, sometimes with a high school class we would prepare a kind of flat bread on a large barbecue grill like an old-fashioned outdoor oven using an indirect cooking technique.

You can start with a chilled pizza dough, either homemade or store bought. Then, we would prepare a vegetarian "hamburger," using fresh ingredients from the garden: Beefsteak tomato slice, onion, basil leaf, and greens. Use pizza dough cut into flat little rounds and cooked on a hot grill, with the coals banked to one side and the little flat breads away from direct heat and in just 4 minutes you have a hot bread.

Using the same table set up as with pie making, 5 eggs to a pound of flour makes pasta dough, in a large stainless steel bowl. The students, first, wash and dry their hands. Similar to pie making, you might have prepared a dough by another class, that has already had some time to rest. You can use a fork or your fingers to make a hole in the flour, crack and add in the eggs, and mix together to make a dough. A sieve is used to sprinkle flour to both dry, clean hands, and to coat the freezer paper that covers the work surface. That dough can be used or set aside to rest.

Five pasta machines are clamped to a cutting board and the table, and the rollers are set on #'s 1-5. The students write their name or initial on a paper plate. Starting at station #1 a small slice of dough is run through the rollers, and folded over and rolled again. The first student takes this slice around the table and rolling it thinner and longer at each station. Soon the whole group is moving around the table much like when dipping beeswax candles. When they reach the 5th station they cut this into sheets that can fit on their plate, and go around again collecting a small stack of pasta sheets. A light dusting of flour keeps things from sticking together.

When everyone has been around three or four times, the handles are taken out of the roller and put into the cutting unit and ribbons of fettuccine can be made at all five stations. Depending on the size of the class, you might have 2-3 students at each machine cutting noodles. Each student's noodles can be lightly tossed with flour in the bowls and bagged up to take home.

Or you can have a large pot of boiling water on the stove and these will cook up in 2 minutes and you can serve them with a little butter and your herb salt. Other times we've dried these in the dehydrator and bagged the up in zip locks to take home.

Once you've become comfortable with making noodles, you will want to share the tactile sense for the "feel of the dough." This is another example of the intelligence that lives in our hands. Typically, this is a developmental path: using the hands for a direct experience; then using a tool, such as a fork (Open hand) and spoon or spade (Closed hand) for endurance and heavier work. Our modern culture tends to bypass our hands for power tools and loses something uniquely human along the way.

Parsnip/Carrot Fries

Another great thing to keep up your sleeve for a cold winter day is homemade, baked french fries. Or better yet, use parsnips and carrots, and with older classes, perhaps, add some onion as well. I find that onions are a rather adult flavor that is more appealing to the older students.

The great thing about carrots and a school garden is pulling just what you need, when you need, and snacking on them raw, or cooking. Parsnips can wait in the ground until February or March even. Carrots tend to rot, particularly if your soil is too heavy and the carrots are left out too long. Many people are not as familiar with parsnips, as they are with carrots. As a matter of fact, before the potato was introduced to Europe, parsnips were *the* winter root vegetable.

To prepare, preheat a hot oven (450) and slice the veggies you want to roast. In a large bowl coat them with a little olive oil and soy sauce and roast on a baking sheet ~20 minutes. To speed things up cut them somewhat thin like french fries. And if you are using potatoes, try one of those hand operated french fry slicers for even sticks. Top with your seasoned salt and serve. Cooking with parchment paper makes clean up easy.

This is not merely a treat, but a genuine experience of taking something from garden to table. Students can copy the recipe from the board, or you can preprint them. They will feel inspired to share that recipe at home reinforcing the circle between student–parent–teacher in a wonderful way.

Beeswax Candles

We have not had surplus beeswax from our own bees, but to make the connection, I order beeswax and wicking from Brushy Mountain Bee Farm and set up to dip candles before Candlemas in early February. I also order sheets of beeswax for rolling candles. They also carry little pearls of beeswax that are great in herbal balms and lotions that we make with the eighth grade.

Setup is similar to the pasta making, in that the whole group will slowly rotate around the table, coming to the two dipping stations along the way. Only it requires more protection: both the floor and the table, to make clean up easier. I have extra-heavy-duty scraps from covering the greenhouse that I use year after year. These heavy-duty sheets worked great. The 6-8 mil thick can be folded up, taken outside and the wax drops pop right off and they can be reused over and over.

Two hot plates, set up with double boilers and tall tins (think: pineapple juice tins) hold the melted beeswax, set inside the pan holding the hot water. By setting the two dipping stations on opposite ends, there is time between dips to cool and make each dip gather a good layer. To avoid getting wax all over the hot plate and double boiler, I make a hood out of foil that is open to the wax, but covers everything else.

An older class can help prepare precut 9" tapers by dipping once and holding straight for 30 seconds. Younger classes than just need to line up and start dipping. If hot plates are not strong: start on the stove; and carefully move over.

Other Kitchen Projects

Tortilla making, corn and/or flour; making butter from cream; juicing, carrots, making a "V8" juice, or different blends of fruit, herbs, and veggies; mini-pizzas or sandwich variations, as described in the Bread/Pasta section.

Late Winter/Early Spring Garden Activities

Spring comes late in USDA Zone 6. Our last frost can vary from March 20 to May 5, with the average around April 17. Although there has been a trend towards earlier last frost dates, it takes just an occasional late frost to swing the average back. That's the thing about averages. More noticeable changes with climate change, are extremes: heavy rains and droughts; hard storms, and heat waves. Gardeners increasingly need to design resilient systems and strategies that incorporate greenhouses, high tunnels, efficient irrigation, mulches, and plant protection covers.

General rules include never sowing all your heirloom seed in one season; staggering your spring plantings; and having supplies close at hand for supplemental irrigation and frost protection.

Coppicing and Pollarding

In winter, you can see the bare bones of the garden and deciduous trees and late winter is the time to prune. This pictures shows the basket willow as a coppice; cut back to ground level every winter. (Except during the first two establishment years.) Pollarding is the same thing, only the plants are cut back to a height above deer-browsing level and were also used outside the garden deer fence, as a windbreak for the prevailing northwest winds.

Note: Safety is always on my mind. When using loppers; both hands are well away from the cutting area. And its easy to maintain a coppice with loppers alone. With saws and hand clippers, there is a greater chance for self-injury. Using gloves at all times when pruning helps provide some protection.

Firewood

The heavier pruning, pollarding with the taller white willow for firewood, proved a great activity for my active high school classes. Previous greenhouse photos show wheelbarrows of firewood that was cut to length green that had yet to be stacked for drying and use in our clay stove. Willow has no splinters.

Forcing Flowers

I also pollard weeping willow, as this gives long, graceful whips that are used in the autumn to make willow stars and wreath circles (easier than grape vine). In February and March, it is possible to make fabulous bouquets using: forsythia, magnolia, pussy willow, and most any prunus; peach, almond, etc. I planted borders of these for just this season's use.

Because the weather is unpredictable, older classes sometimes pick buckets of branches for putting together bouquets indoors. Then if the weather was awful, we had the material indoors already. As soon as these branches experience a certain number of hours above 45 degrees at night, they start to bloom. It's that dynamic of seeing a dormant twig burst into beauty that awakens appreciation for nature's hidden secrets.

Any size bouquets can be made from these, from small 12" bunches, to 60" displays used during school plays or on stage for assemblies. Some years, we would have beautiful indoor displays while there is still snow outside and spring still seems just a distant dream.

Later, fresh flower bouquets naturally come in, including daffodils, narcissus, hyacinth, tulip, and more. We wrap these bunches using a rubber band, paper towel, and plastic wrap to make a portable bouquet that could travel home with a student and stay moist. Masking tape gives a great surface for writing names or initials on the bouquet.

Parents love having these "ambassadors of spring" find their way home in the hands of their eager children. Many bulbs have flowering stems that can be plucked by hand without clippers, as this fifth grade group is doing.

Spring Garden Activities

Spring can be a short season in zone 6. Dancing around the May Pole on May Day is a school tradition to mark this time of year. Often the old large magnolia trees have bloomed quietly over spring break going unnoticed, or caught by spring frosts leaving a blanket of blooms decaying all around, like an echo of autumn nourishing the earth.

I've skipped many gardening points, because I assume you are already a gardener and there are many other resource books for that. But during April and May, your attention shifts towards getting the annual summer garden planted to carry over a wave of momentum into next school year.

This means, depending upon you facilities, you've started flats of annuals for transplanting as soon as weather and facility permits. Using our own soil blends, mostly 1:3 Perlite to sifted compost, our seedlings have a lot of "cling." That means the roots have plenty of hairs that cling to the soil mix, making transplanting easy. I use a triple-tray system, in the standard 10" x 20" size with: A) carrying trays around the B) seedling flat inserted into a C) solid 10 x 20 tray to hold water. This prevents leakage for trays indoors, yet you can lift out the carrying tray that gives extra support to the, often, flimsy seedling flat, if you need to drain out excess water. This means you can water from below and have little or no spillage. Every gardener has their own system.

I also use wooden tags and clear domes. The domes make a greenhouse in a greenhouse and increase the humidity speeding germination. In addition to the 128 cell germination trays, I also use the 2" round cells, with and without peat pot liners. Peat pots are handy, allowing for easy consolidation of trays, or planting mixed herb, flower, or salad bowls, and for selling.

Windowsill space is limited, so I often use the 128 flats indoors, later transplanting to the 2", 4 x 8 cell 32 trays,

which can be moved outside (either to cold frames and later after it was built: to the cool greenhouse) for further protection and growing on prior to transplanting directly in the garden.

October to June

Before building a greenhouse, I used cold frames on black drums filled with water for thermal mass as a protected propagation area. Here, I could move transplanted trays with their domes from inside to out. Without any supplemental heating, this protected tomato seedlings down to 27 degrees one April. But that year it was fatal for the watermelon seedlings.

Once you have a system for raising seedlings, you can branch out into different ways for using them. In addition to getting the annual beds of your garden entirely planted during the month of May, you may have extra seedlings for further projects. I've found the hanging 10" pots useful for vertical gardening in the greenhouse. You can even get extension hangers so that you can hang a double row from the same rafter, for an efficient two-tier, vertical growing space in your greenhouse.

I've already mentioned, that rather than having separate square foot gardens for different classes, we treat the garden as a shared community project. Yet throughout the year, students have taken home things from the garden, thus making it more personal. I do this in springtime by planting individual 10" hanging pots for each student to take home before Mother's Day weekend. The sixth grade would take home a "salad garden" filled with edible greens, the seventh grade would take home a "flower bowl" and the eighth grade would take home an "herb bowl."

These first two bowls use seedlings and the third uses cuttings started around April 15. The 10" hanging bowl fits into a plastic shopping bag for easy transport with or without the hanger. This takes a similar process and adds variation for the different class groups, as well as something to look forward to, as they see the other classes take home bowls with their name tags. (Make a few extra, in case of failure, or for the class teacher.)

Double row on right, hanging from same rafter.

Every garden teacher imagines beds neatly planted, and even though free-form patterns is very organic, rows help students see what's intended and what's a weed, while leaving room for cultivation and mulching. To help form this, I made planting sticks. I took thirty-two, 3" lag bolts and "planted" them in the same 2", 32-cell planting tray I plant in.

Bury the hex head, with the screw end facing up, in a sifted fence-post, quick-set concrete mix. Wear a dust mask while sifting. Use two carrying trays for support underneath, the 32-cell tray and sprinkle with a gentle water source, allowing air bubbles to surface (don't fill all the way just like with plants) and adjust any lag bolts so the screws are facing straight up. Let that set overnight.

Take a 32" long, 2" x 2" bannister stick, and pre-drill guide holes, slightly smaller than the diameter of the lag screws, at intervals you like. I used 6" intervals, giving me combinations of 6, 12, 18, and 24 inches. The first time you screw in the cement "popsicle," you are shaping the threading inside the wooden planting stick that will allow you to change spacing, as you need.

In soft soil, you simply press it in, and you have perfectly spaced and sized holes for transplanting.

I made eight of these planting sticks allowing for different combinations. If I was planting a bed where every 12" there was a row of 5 plants 6" apart running perpendicular to the path, I would go down the edge of the path with the 12" planting stick marking a row of guide holes, than a student, or pair of students could use the 6" sticks to mark out each cross-row of five planting holes.

Now all you need to do is bring out the flats for transplanting and drop your seedlings, with or without peat pots, directly into a well-proportioned grid with in a bed. If the seedlings are large enough, you can have leaf mulch close at hand and presto, an instant bed with a strong chance of getting established ahead of weed growth. The same technique can be used with un-sprouted or pre-sprouted onion sets, potatoes. With grains, 5 seeds per cell, sown 3-4 weeks earlier, and with wheat, rye, spelt, or barley, you quickly fill a bed.

Bed Preparation

There are many different approaches I've incorporated into a school garden, from double-digging by hand with high schoolers, to using a tiller to quickly prepare a bed. However you do it, the bottom line is soil health. It's easy to overwork the soil. It needs compost, cover crops, and crop rotation.

Other books cover this well. Having run a 10-acre farm CSA for five years, I know that many practices are shaped by the choice of tools.

In that case: tractors and traditional farm equipment. Across the street, on school property is a farm and a CSA, so for the annual section of the school garden I left enough room for a tractor to come in, should the need arise. Once during the early years this was helpful.

I've learned never to paint myself into a corner. Leave yourself room to drive a pickup truck just about anywhere in, or around the garden for deliveries, or hauling materials.

Earlier pictures in the Annual Garden Beds and Cover Crops section, shows many of the steps in getting the garden ready for May plantings. Similar to my CSA days, I used a 5', on center, measurement for bed layout. This works for hand or tractor cultivation and helps in record keeping.

At the time, you think you will remember everything, but take a lot of pictures with date stamps. The picture below, around August 1, shows tilling in a summer cover crop of buckwheat.

You have time to sow another cover. Oats or annual rye can double as pathway (mow if needed) and the cover crop can be tilled in before planting winter cover crop. In the background are two 10' gates in for tractor access and 8' tall perimeter deer fencing to protect the garden.

6 Sustainability — Nature and Society

Sustainability — Program and Personal

I used to think of sustainability only in environmental terms, such as in forestry: Only harvest as much as what the landscape can replenish. Later, I came to see it also in human and economic terms, as well as in an ecological-balancing dynamic. It's tempting to think teachers have it easy...but it's not a career for everyone. The demands are emotional, physical, and economic. A weakness in anyone of these three areas can be a deal breaker for sustaining your teaching career and your growing garden.

Saving Your Sanity

Although a whole topic unto itself, you need to find a way to sustain your whole self. A danger is: *Do the impossible and it becomes your job description*. The reason the school day ends early, is in part because teachers have so much to do in terms of lesson preparation. And for the garden teacher, a certain amount of reparation is needed, including garden maintenance.

This takes time and reflection. This reparation is not only correcting any mistakes a class may have done, but the self-education that comes from reflecting back over how a lesson went, and how you would like to do better, or different next time.

In garden teaching, sustainability includes, how to repeat lessons/activities, more easily in the future, than it might have been the first time you did it. There is nothing like a teacher's first year. Ideally, you get the chance to see a master teacher in action during your training and get first hand experience in how they've found sustainable strategies that work.

A big part of what teachers do is set the stage wherein learning moments occur. Often this means being awake in the moment. Knowing what is the right lesson, for a particular age group, is where the strength of a good curriculum comes in.

Teachers also carry an invisible emotional weight, as they wonder how to support children who struggle or are troubled. Often these struggles are rooted outside of school, yet carry over into the school day. Sometimes, you can follow up with other teachers, or the parents. Nonetheless, it is a good practice to carry positive thoughts of the student into your evening meditations, and more often than not, you are rewarded with fresh inspiration the next morning on how to work with an individual.

In addition to a lesson book, where you make notes about attendance and individuals, keep a journal with all your questions, and observations, for your own benefit. This will strengthen your passion about your work, save your sanity, and feed your spirit.

Budget

Although this will vary for every situation, every school garden has two aspects to its budget: short term consumables that are used up in the course of teaching and longer term expenditures that have will lasting benefit, such as tools and equipment. Perhaps you have the luxury of having both an operating and a capital budget, but if you don't, you will try to do the best for both, out of your line item budget.

Consumables might include first aid supplies, cooking supplies, packaging, crafting supplies, office supplies, paper, pencils, mulch, compost, annual seeds, nursery pots, trays and containers, etc.

Capital items include things that might last 8 years or more, such as tools, equipment, garden structures, perennial plants: herbs, trees, bulbs, berries, shrubs, etc.

Tools and Work Strategies

I was not able to acquire all the tools I needed the first year, and continued to add tools each year as my budget allowed and as capacities evolved. If we think of a sequential garden curriculum, you might proceed from the hands-on experiences, and gradually introduce manual tools, and possibly include power tools that fit your curriculum and age group.

Again refer back to the first chapter, what is gardening for, because *tools determine: what you do; who does what; and with what efficiency.* You want to match your tools with your desired age-appropriate outcome. Occasionally I would leave a push reel type lawn mower out: and someone with excess energy would, unasked give a go at it.

For the child under sixth grade, you want to engage the hands. Like the 4-H motto of head, heart, hands, and health: you want a sense connection with nature and community. Before I could afford wheelbarrows, I made stretchers from recycled materials. These could be carried by four third-graders, or two fifth-graders. It seems silly to use a wheelbarrow to haul autumn leaves to the compost shed: use a tarp or stretcher instead.

After sixth grade, see how: the spade, or trowel, is the closed hand; and the fork or cultivator is the open hand, with fingers! Early tool development is an extension of the hand, into wood, metal, or stone, to sustain greater work capacities. Even a wheelbarrow is like an arm full, extended out, into a barrow or stretcher.

That said, gloves are an early addition to your tool shed. Children's hands are very tender and the option to cover up is good. But most won't want to, they long to connect with the world, while others will appreciate a little distance. Later as work gets heavier, gloves will be more important. Needless to say, first aid supplies must be handy. Injuries on the sports field or play ground are not uncommon. But that need not carry over to the garden.

Large seeds, beans, corn, squash, and onion and potato sets, can all be planted by hand. While older students might use a tool for seeding smaller seeds in a tray, or directly in the garden.

My classes varied from 8-16 students at a time. I try to add new tools each year, to be divided up among the four, color-coded groups. One year it might be: Hand trowels and weeders; watering cans; buckets and baskets; leaf rakes; spades and forks; garden rakes; loppers; hand clippers; grafting knives; shovels; wheelbarrows; etc. I would get 16 of each, or 8 one year and 8 more the next, depending on what the budget could allow. I could not afford to get everything I needed the first year, so added something every year as the garden grew.

Sometimes a class needs to pull together and work closer. Other times, people need their space, peace, and independence, and to spread out. Tools and work strategies can give you the flexibility to respond to these different needs on the fly. Sometimes you might want to ask an individual, or couple to do a special task over here...other times a kind of playful competition arises and teams are trying to outdo each other pushing wheelbarrows or carrying stretchers. By getting, and putting away, all the tools in their right place, you reinforce a sense of order and respect. Take all the time needed to do this early on, and it will serve everyone well.

Cultural Sustainability

It's easy to over extend yourself when you are establishing, maintaining, and developing, an educational garden. I often say, "The garden is for the younger child and by the older." Nonetheless, as soon as they become confident capable gardeners:

65

they graduate! And as a teacher, you are constantly teaching new comers.

Yet, if you have the chance to team up your older students, as mentors to the younger, you will see how gardening can become part of the culture of a school, as familiar as any recess game. I found this one of the most satisfying accomplishments in the school garden: older students working side-by-side with younger. Something vital passes between the two groups that I as a teacher cannot provide, yet can facilitate.

You can extend this, to the realm of parent volunteers. Typically parents of younger children are more available than of older children. You might be able to get parent volunteers in pre-k, kindergarten, or after school programs. As children detach from parental bonds, you might be able to steer a parent away from just the class their child is in to help with another class. Using parent volunteers has its challenges and rewards. If there is a teacher already using volunteers in their class, ask them for advice. Your administration might help coordinate volunteers as well.

Join a garden teacher group. I did in Northern California and found it very helpful. It was a revelation to discover that everyone struggles with similar issues. It's not just my problem!

7 Curriculum

Learning Moment

There is magic in the moment of learning. Sometimes it is called the Ah-ha moment of discovery. Much of our work as teachers is to set up lessons and activities so that students make discoveries for themselves.

There is an art of setting the stage for this meeting between where the student is at, and how they encounter the world, or an idea. Some call it "building a fire." It's a kind of eureka moment.

In addition to gardening, it was a geometry teacher who first showed me that discovery is a delight that fuels ones' quest for knowledge. He was using a calculator, and a smile burst over his face when he saw the answer, and he laughed aloud. There is beauty in ratios, proportions, and mathematics. And there is confidence in knowing the truth. Much of the enthusiasm common to all scientists is rooted in this experience. Every child is an artist and scientist, because we are capable of discovery.

You can't repeat a first impression. There is something singular, unique, and genuine in each moment of discovery. Having seen it once, it's not the same a second time. As a teacher you will model the wonder, awe, and joy that lives within every discovery. The best way, of course, is to always be ready for such discoveries yourself. My enthusiasm for teaching is rooted in my love of learning.

As a subject teacher, the more you know what the children are learning in other classes and main lessons, appropriate to their age, the more you will know what they are ready to discover in your gardening classes. We see what we are ready to see.

Through the Grades

Third Grade

The theme of farming and our relationship to domestic livestock and grains plays a big part in the third grade. The students have the opportunity to grow wheat, corn, beans, potatoes, onions, and many other crops that bring them closer to understanding where our daily food comes from and how we depend upon the work of others every day.

Here they begin to learn simple gardening tasks and the value of working cooperatively. Developmentally they still bring a lot of joy to everything they do, such that one could say they work playfully. In this way, a seed is planted for much later in life—the joy of being of service others. I feel this is the true purpose of work.

Each autumn the third grade class harvests corn. The children count the number of kernels in a row, and the number of rows, and find that there are over 400 kernels on each of the two or three ears that each plant produces. They are amazed to learn that it only takes one seed to grow a plant that provides nearly a thousand more kernels or seeds. At the same time, they practice chanting the times tables in main lesson—The power of multiplication.

Thus, it takes the seeds from just two ears to grow almost two thousand more ears of corn. Amid such a harvest, we set aside seed corn for next year's crop—as we have done years. This seed corn is different from the rest of the harvest, because it is meant for someone else. Now we can perhaps understand what the Native Americans meant, when in the ceremony of presenting corn to another tribe, they declared, "Here, all the food you shall ever need, if you but tend it properly."

The seed corn the third graders set aside is for next year's third-grade class. This seed comes from the seed planted by the previous third-grade class, which comes from the seed planted by the third-grade class before that, and so on. Experiencing the grain in this way, the children see that it is not just a thing but a living giving being. Each year we begin with the seed, and, after the harvest is consumed, we end with the seed—the Alpha and the Omega.

We grow an open-pollinated variety of corn called Calico. This type of corn has kernels of many colors, but each kernel pops white. It's always a surprise to see what colors lie hidden underneath the white or purple husks.

Fifth, Sixth, and Seventh Grade

At Kimberton, gardening continues fifth grade through tenth. In the fifth grade, they have a botany main lesson block in the spring as well as the Greek Games. This is a time of beautiful balance in body and soul.

By the sixth grade they plunge deeper into the physical world and study geology and physics including cause and effect. It's a challenge to have the children experience the full growing season, since they are on break during the summer. So one has to be patient; not all discoveries happen within class hours.

Nonetheless, we experience the cycles of nature and find that to everything there is a season. The sixth-grade students help make compost from grass clippings, leaves, and from kitchen scraps from the school's organic lunch program. Together we make about seven yards of compost a year.

The fact that waste, sometimes rather foul, can be transformed into good soil is a powerful lesson: Making lemonade from lemons.

Every sixth grade plants some perennials, in addition to tending the annual plantings. One year they planted pear trees, another year apple trees, raspberry bushes, and so on. After each class planted these, we say a verse given me by Richard St. Barbe Baker, the English Forester: *When I plant a tree, I am a servant of God. And faces that I've not met, Shall call me blessed.*

One year, after they had stood back and looked at their planting pride, a student asked, "When do we get apples?"

"Oh, real soon," I replied, "in about four years."

"Four years! I'll be in tenth grade by then."

"I certainly hope so."

They really don't know how long it takes. Through this planting, the students learn patience and realize that their actions contribute to the future. They learn, too, that we depend on others, many of whom we have never met and worked long ago for our benefit.

This is traditional agriculture. Honor those who came before; respect those who will follow.

Middle schoolers also have a chance to take home herbs, flowers, potatoes, carrots, and tomatoes from the garden. An important dynamic takes place when the circle between parent, teacher and student reinforces a love for learning, creativity, and work. This is food for the soul.

Eighth Grade

In eighth grade, we work with medicinal plants making a simple salve from lavender, plantain, olive oil, and beeswax. We also become familiar with local poisonous plants: pokeweed, horse nettle, poison ivy, and others. We also have picked, washed, and packed some garden produce for a local food bank. Thus our work reaches the wider world. This is half of the inner calling of the farmer: *Feed the hungry! The other half is: Tend and heal the Earth that feeds us!*

Ninth Grade

In the ninth grade, we explore the ideas behind organic practices and the social issues of land use and stewardship. We double dig some garden beds, looking at soil stratas. We study the history of the Dustbowl in the 1930s and the formation, and work, of the Civilian Conservation Corps and the Soil Conservation Service. We also study the Ag. Conservation

Easement legislation written by a founding School Board member of the Kimberton Waldorf school and PA State Representative Samuel Morris, for whom our Garden building is named. Students also work at a host farm during a 2-week practicum in the spring.

Tenth Grade and the High School Gardening Elective

In the tenth grade more advanced horticultural skills, such as grafting fruit trees, are introduced and practiced. The high school elective students help to develop the garden as a whole and assist with projects in progress by younger classes.

71

The first school experience for many children is in a kindergarten or children's garden. During my years as a gardening teacher, I have seen that it is, not the plants per se, but the students who do the most growing in the garden. Whereas corn always brings forth corn, the children each season bring something new to the garden and into the world.

In them lies hope for the future. A good education seeks to grow learners eager to learn more, sometimes called a love for life-long learning. The more we learn, the more we learn there is to know. Keeping an open mind is the door to discovery.

8 Conclusion

The long and continuing road in establishing gardening as an essential practice in education. The earth is always trying to heal itself. The question is: Are we part of that healing or are we contributing to further injury?

The first Waldorf School arose in response to the devastating effects following the First World War. The question then was: What would be the best way to get society on a healthy footing? How could the fullest capacities of the human being be nurtured and brought out?

The Waldorf Curriculum arose during this creative time and included gardening in the 6-10th grade curriculum. Shortly after the founding of the first Waldorf School, a similar impulse towards healing our relationship towards agriculture, and the land that supports us, known as biodynamics.

This was all disrupted, to put it mildly, with the events leading up to WWII. The Nazis hated the Waldorf Schools and shut them down. The Kimberton Waldorf School opened in 1941 with the plan of accepting fleeing refugee children, yet the transport ship was sunk, and the school shifted its focus to local students.

The war effort transformed American Industry and Agriculture into a powerhouse. Yet, huge environmental costs from radioactive and chemical pollution remained unappreciated for decades. In the 1950s, above-ground nuclear testing resulted in radioactive isotopes showing up in milk, from fallout on grass and concentrated by grazing cattle. Above ground test bans eventually followed. Later, Rachel Carson documented how agricultural chemicals can go through a process of biomagnification and lead to unintended health consequences.

She died of breast cancer shortly after publishing *Silent Spring*. Scientific research continues, albeit slowly, into the many ways human actions continue to have unintended environmental consequences. Endangered honeybees and climate change show how this is one of the most important situations facing the habitability of our planet and the fate of humanity.

In short, the vision of a school garden is to awaken your conscience, such that you hear the call: Heal the Earth—Serve Humanity and feel moved to become part of the solution. To arrive at that place, requires time and experience. That has been my hope in leading classes through their years in a school garden.

In traditional cultures, this was/is carried by the Elders, the ones who know the laws of nature and our duty as stewards. In recent years, our relationship with nature has become increasingly destructive. We might also reverse destruction and hear this call to Heal Humanity—Serve the Earth.

What I have discovered while teaching gardening is that both tasks are needed. We can't do the one without the other. If we want to heal the earth, we must bring a new impulse into education— including our relationship with the earth. And if we want the best education, we need the life-giving forces that come through the earth, particularly the Plant Kingdom.

"We learn with the same forces we grow with." —Rudolf Steiner

In order to be ready to learn, we need to be well nourished.

"A hungry man is an angry man." — Bob Marley

A healthy lunch program, and possibly even a breakfast program, makes sense in educational settings where busy parents need help in creating the best learning environment possible during these early years of human development.

There is something of a Catch-22 challenge. Without a gardening program we won't know the need for one. Nonetheless, this barrier will come down as more schools learn by doing, and discover gardening is much more than soil, plants, and animals, but people too. A gardening program educates students through practical experience that we as human beings draw our daily sustenance from the earth, and therefore have responsibilities towards the earth and the well being of others.

Gardening also strengthens our sense of hope, as we experience how our efforts actually do make a positive difference: seeds sprout and grow; compost improves soil, and good soil grows good things. This is how gardening is a metaphor towards building healthy communities.

Gardening teaches not only horticulture, but also kindles the human spirit through something we might call the "metamorphosis of the soul."—Interest awakens responsibilities, later this ripens into love for the world. At which point, they have become elders themselves. During a validation circle with a senior class, one student shared that she felt like a plant, well cared for in our school garden. It was then that I learned what garden teaching is really all about.

We can call these educational gardens: "Gardens that grow people." I envision a future where every K-12 school will have two, full-time gardening teachers tending to young students and the environment we thrive in.

9 Appendices

Through The Year

Along with your class attendance lists, it's a good to plan an outline of the year anticipating vacations, parent conferences, festivals, field trips, term changes, and reporting periods. Again, this is very individual to your school and teaching assignments. In addition to teaching gardening in the high school and lower grades, I taught botany and earth science in the high school, while advising individuals and a high school class, and coordinating a farm practicum in the high school.

I prepare a binder at the beginning of the year, with sections for each class, including student lists, lesson plans, and blank pages to make quick notes after each class. Time is tight, so often a single word, or note, by each students name after a class helps when it comes time, twice a year, to write brief reports for parent conferences. Everyone has their own system.

As I hinted at earlier, in nearly every class we are reaping, or using, something planted months earlier, while setting something aside for later classes. And because of the academic year, this often carries over from one calendar year to the next., as when third graders begin the year harvesting dry corn planted by this years' fourth grade class. They too will be very different students in just seven months, when they plant the saved seed, for next year's third grade.

Gradually, this grows into a school-wide cultural phenomena, as everyone eventually has a hand in the garden.

September–Harvest

Nursery–Sift compost and store for soil mixes

Greenhouse–Weeding, cleaning and organizing

Garden–Harvest Indian popcorn, separate stalks, ears, and store corn, harvest herbs and flowers for drying, sow spelt, wheat, and rye, in flats for transplanting 3 weeks later

Fruits

Harvest berries; dry some as well for herb tea blend.

Classroom–Finish drying herbs, flowers, and fruits

Herb Salt

Herb Tea,

Paperwork–Organize tools groups, and class schedules.

October–Harvest

Nursery–Sift compost and store for soil mixes

Greenhouse–Weeding, cleaning and organizing

Garden–Harvest Indian Popcorn, separate stalks, ears, and store corn Harvesting herbs and flowers for drying Sow spelt, wheat, and rye in flats for transplanting 3 weeks later

Fruits

Harvest berries; dry some as well for herb tea blend. Classroom

Finish drying herbs, flowers, and fruits

Herb Salt

Herb Tea,

Paperwork–Organize tools groups, and class schedules.

November–Thanksgiving

Nursery–Gathering & stockpiling leaves for compost, year-round composting

Greenhouse Monitoring–Watering, venting, warming monitoring bulb bowls

Garden–Final cover cropping, mulching, and putting the garden to bed

Fruits

Pruning as weather permits

Classroom Cooking; Pumpkin pies

Herb Salt

Herb Tea

Paperwork–Parent teacher conference summaries and comments

December–Advent and Craft Show

Nursery–Ordering containers for indoors; trays, domes, etc.

Greenhouse Monitoring–Watering, venting, warming monitoring bulb bowls, paperwhites for craft show

Garden–Harvesting greens for wreaths, make willow stars for craft show

Fruits

Pruning as weather permits

Classroom cooking, Christmas cookies

Candle making: dip or rolled beeswax

Herb Salt

Herb Tea

Paperwork

Ordering seeds, containers, and supplies

January–Return from Winter Break

Nursery–Gathering containers for indoors, trays, domes, etc.

Greenhouse Monitoring–Watering, venting, warming sowings in window sills indoors, soil mix, stored over winter in barrels

Garden–Cutting willow for firewood and storing in greenhouse

Fruits

Pruning as weather permits

Classroom Cooking–Making pasta noodles, sowings, first sowings of peppers, tomatoes, chamomile, onion, statice etc.

Candlemaking

Herb Salt

Herb Tea

Paperwork–Going over catalogs and orders

February–Presidents Weekend

Nursery–Send home bulb bowls; freesia, anemone, and ranunculus.

Greenhouse monitoring; watering, venting, warming, Potting-on as needed

Sowings–basil, strawflowers, gomphrena, etc.

Soil mix

Garden–Willow pruning, harvesting branches for forcing flowers, forsythia, magnolia, etc.

Coppice and pollarding

Fruits

Pruning–Save any wood for grafting

Classroom Cooking–Apple pies, pumpkin pies,

Sowings & potting-on

Herb Salt

Herb Tea

Paperwork–Winter Conferences PASA

March–Spring Break

Nursery–Turning, shredding & compost for new bin space

Greenhouse monitoring; watering, venting, warming

Potting-on, as needed

Sowings

Soil mix

Garden–Willow weaving

Pruning Coppice and Pollarding

Burn piles

Charcoal Making

Fruits–Pruning and save any wood for grafting

Classroom Cooking–Tortillias, Salsa, Parsnip fries,

Sowings–Potting-on

Herb Salt

Herb Tea

Paperwork

Parent Conference summaries and comments

April–Earth Day

Nursery Potting-on peat-pots

Sowings

Soil mix

Graft fruit trees

Garden Tilling

Top dressing

Branches/Pruning

Clean-up

Harvest flowers for kitchen and bouquets for students to take home

Mulching

Frost protection over tender herbs, corn, peppers & tomatoes, as needed

Sow grass seed to fill-in any lawn bare patches

Fruits

Weeding Berries

Staking

Biodynamic tree paint application

Classroom Sowings

Potting-on

Herb Salt

Herb Tea

Dig parsnips that have over wintered in ground for "fries"

Paperwork

State Order

May–May Day

Nursery Planting out

Seedlings and bowls for students to take home

Herbs, vegetables, flowers, tomatoes, etc.

Garden

Cut cover crop and make compost

Planting out Weeding/cultivating around new transplants

Mulching beds

Trellis set-up for tomatoes, cucumbers, and beans

Gather dry grass-clippings for mulch

Direct sow carrots, annual herbs and greens.

Paperwork

Year end report summaries

June–Graduation

Nursery Planting out

Garden–Cut cover crop and make compost

Planting out

Weeding/cultivating around new transplants

Mulching beds

Trellis set-up for tomatoes, cucumbers, and beans

Fruits

Mulching Berries, staking and tying; spray or bag apples

Classroom

Accommodate activities in Garden Building; Alums, etc.

Paperwork

Year end report summaries

Summer may involve hosting summer programs and general garden maintenance.

Garden Building

10 Equipment, Utensils, Supplies, & Tools

2 9-Tray Dehydrators, Mortar & Pestle Sets, Blender, Portable Dishwasher–Donated for sterilizing utensils, JD Electric Ride-on Mower, Fan–Large Floor model for ventilation

6 Wooden Desk/Tables, Seats 2-6 depending on configuration, 2 Small Tables, Seats 2-3, 30 Chairs, 2 Teachers' Desks in office

1 Copier/fax/scanner, Wooden bench, 2 Glass door cabinets, 3 Open-shelf cabinets

2 Rolling Library Carts, 2 Library Glass Display Cabinets, 8 Dissecting Scopes, 1 Rolling Chalk Board, 1 Rolling Metal Shelf, Assortment of Garden Reference Books

Kitchen Utensils

4 Pasta Makers, 18 Wooden Cutting Boards, 10 Plastic Cutting Boards, 8 Apple Slicer/Corers, 4 Sets of Measuring Cups &

Spoons, Small metal bowls, Large metal bowls, 4 Cooking pots, Knives, 20 Coffee mugs Assortment of Silverware, 4 Baking sheets, 4 Muffin pans, Can opener, 4 Hot Pads, 1 Electric Griddle, 2 Electric Burners–good for candle dipping

Consumable Supplies

First Aid Supplies Pencils Sharpies Masking Tape Paper, Rubber Bands Florist's Tape & Wire Plastic Bags, Paper Bags, Flour, Eggs, Salt, Spices, Oil, Parchment Paper, Seeds, Homegrown dried: Peppers, Herbs & Flowers and Fruits. Peat Pots, Perlite, Peat Moss, Sand, Lime

Garden Shed Tools

Trowels Weeders, C-shaped Leaf Rakes, Clippers, Loppers, Spades, Forks, Garden Rakes, Sieves, Baskets, Buckets, Hedge clippers, Shears, Hand Slippers, Saws, Wheelbarrows, Hula Hoes, Wire Brushes

Power tools

Belt Sander, Bench Grinder, BCS Garden Tiller

26120384R00056

Made in the USA
Middletown, DE
19 November 2015